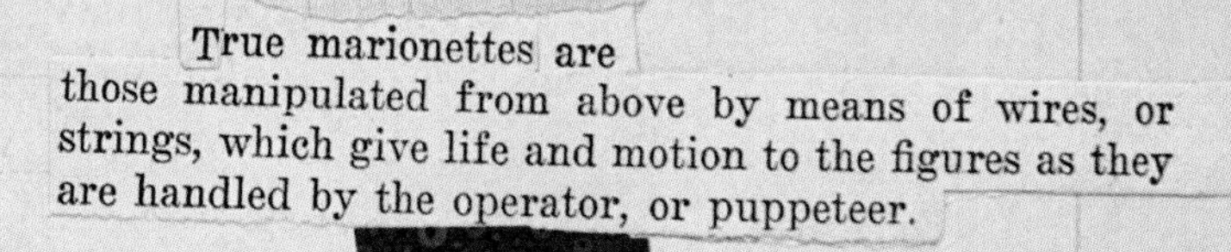

True marionettes are those manipulated from above by means of wires, or strings, which give life and motion to the figures as they are handled by the operator, or puppeteer.

Houghton Mifflin Books for Children is an imprint of Houghton Mifflin Harcourt Publishing Company.

www.hmhco.com

The text of this book is set in Museo.
The illustrations are gouache, collage, and mixed media.
Book design by Rachel Newborn
Production supervision by Crystal Paquette

Library of Congress Cataloging-in-Publication Data

Sweet, Melissa, 1956–
Balloons over Broadway : the true story of the puppeteer of Macy's Parade / by Melissa Sweet.
p. cm.
ISBN 978-0-547-19945-0
1. Sarg, Tony, 1882–1942—Juvenile literature. 2. Puppeteers—United States—Biography—Juvenile literature. 3. Thanksgiving Day—New York (State)—New York—History—Juvenile literature. 4. Parades—New York (State)—New York—History—Juvenile literature.
I. Title.
PN1982.S27S84 2011
791.5'3092—dc22
[B]

2010044181

Manufactured in USA
PHX 4500816050

BALLOONS OVER BROADWAY

The True Story of the Puppeteer of Macy's Parade

WRITTEN AND ILLUSTRATED BY
MELISSA SWEET

Houghton Mifflin Books for Children
HOUGHTON MIFFLIN HARCOURT
Boston New York

Sarg rhymes with aargh!

1880 – 1942

Every little 

Movement has a meaning of its own.

—TONY SARG

From the time he was a little boy, Tony Sarg loved to figure out how to make things move. He once said he became a marionette man when he was only six years old.

His father had asked him to feed their chickens at six-thirty in the morning—every day. Tony had an idea—what if he could feed the chickens without leaving his bed?

He rigged up some pulleys and ran rope from the chicken coop door to his bedroom window. That night, he spread chicken feed outside the chicken coop door.

The next morning . . .

Tony pulled on the rope, and the door to the chicken coop opened!

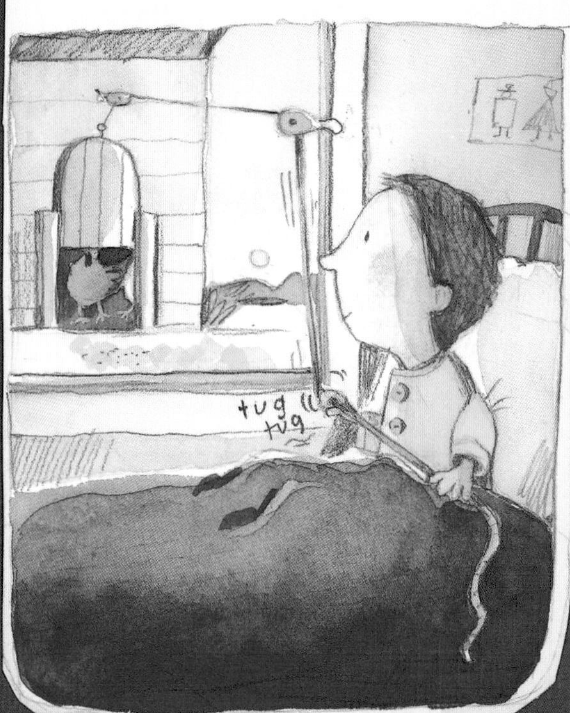

The chickens ate their breakfast, Tony stayed snug in his bed, and his dad, so impressed, never made Tony do another chore.

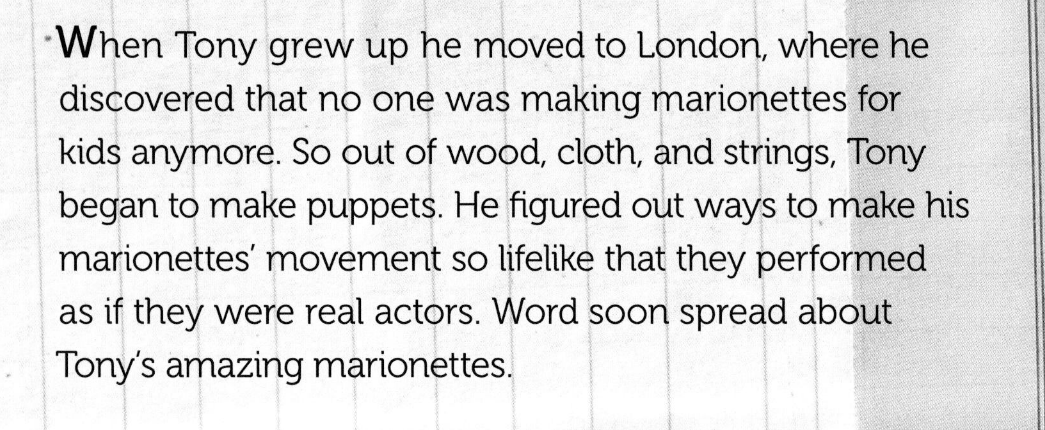

When Tony grew up he moved to London, where he discovered that no one was making marionettes for kids anymore. So out of wood, cloth, and strings, Tony began to make puppets. He figured out ways to make his marionettes' movement so lifelike that they performed as if they were real actors. Word soon spread about Tony's amazing marionettes.

When Tony moved to New York City, the Tony Sarg Marionettes began performing on Broadway.

In the heart of New York City, in Herald Square, was "the biggest store on earth": R. H. Macy's department store. Macy's had heard about Tony's puppets and asked him to design a "puppet parade" for the store's holiday windows. So Tony made new puppets based on storybook characters, then attached them to gears and pulleys to make them move.

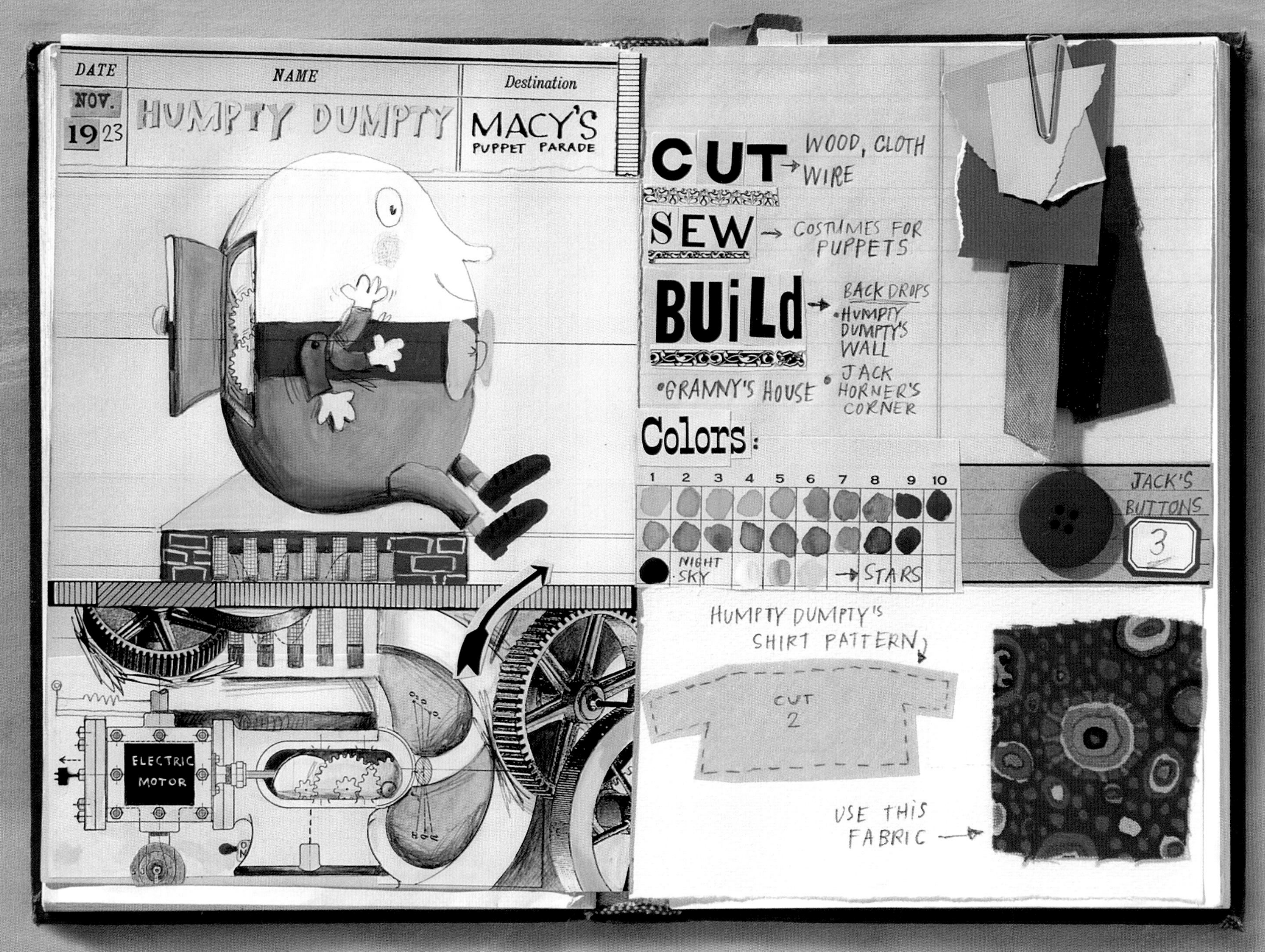

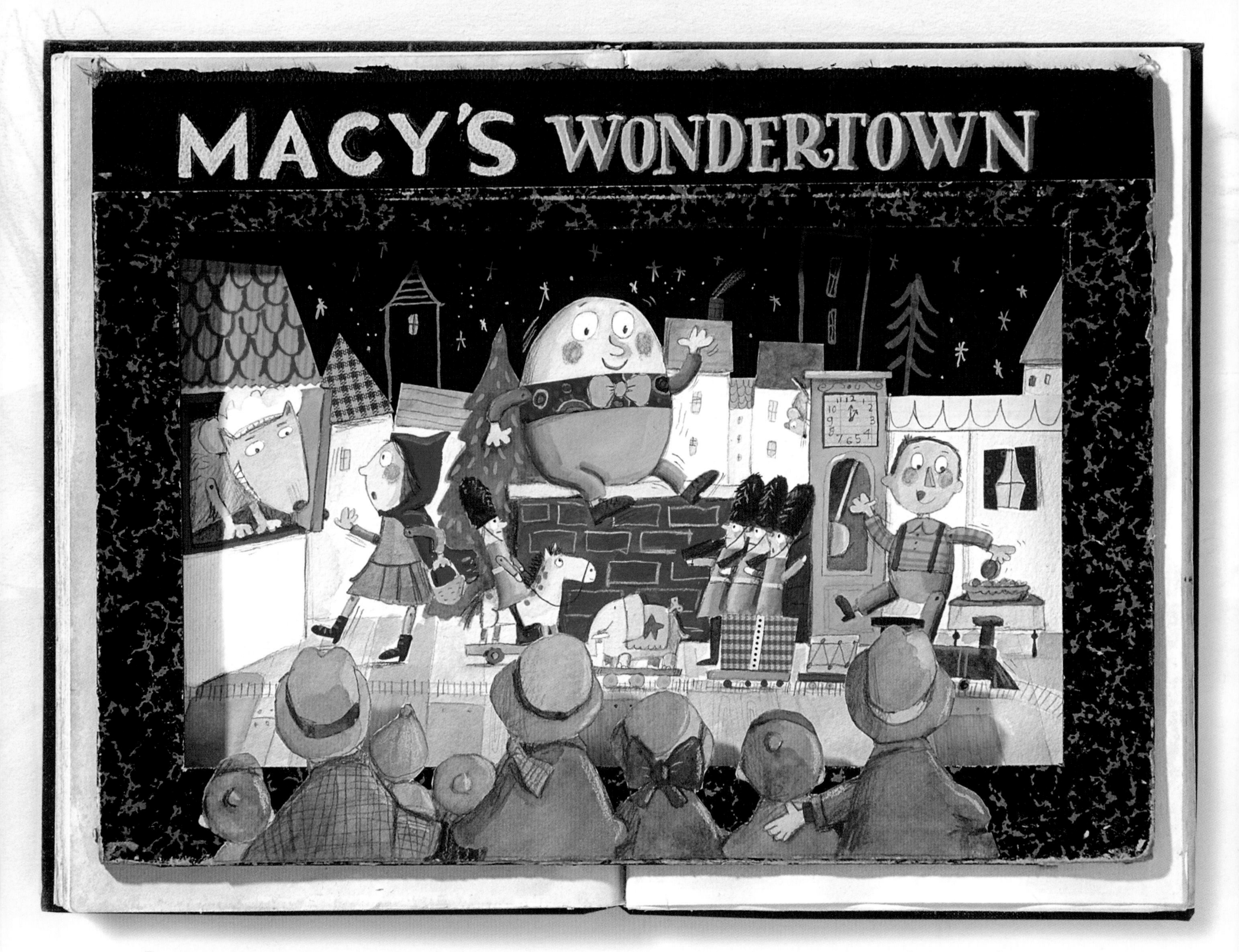

In Macy's "Wondertown" windows, Tony's mechanical marionettes danced across the stage as if by magic. All day long they performed to shoppers jostling for a better look.

But Macy's had an even bigger job in store for Tony.

Many of the people working at Macy's were immigrants, and as the holidays approached, they missed their own holiday traditions of music and dancing in the streets. Macy's agreed to put on a parade for their employees, and they hired Tony to help.

Tony too was an immigrant, so he loved the idea of creating a parade based on street carnivals from all over the world. He made costumes and built horse-drawn floats, and Macy's even arranged to bring in bears, elephants, and camels from the Central Park Zoo.

The animals joined hundreds of Macy's employees on Thanksgiving Day, 1924, winding their way from Harlem to Herald Square. It was a dazzling parade!

In fact, Macy's first parade was such a success that they decided to have one every year on Thanksgiving Day—to celebrate America's own holiday.

Each year the parade grew. But when Macy's brought in lions and tigers—in addition to the bears, elephants, and camels—the animals roared and growled and frightened the children.

Macy's asked Tony to replace the animals.

Tony hoped to replace the animals with some kind of puppets, but his marionettes were less than three feet tall. He would have to make much larger puppets in order for them to be seen in the parade. And how could he make them strong enough to hold up in bad weather yet light enough to move up and down the streets?

Tony knew of a company in Ohio that made blimps out of rubber—the perfect material for any weather. When he called the company and showed them his sketches, they agreed to make what Tony wanted.

Still, how would Tony make his big puppets *move?*

Then Tony had an idea—from an Indonesian rod puppet in his toy collection.

On Thanksgiving Day, Tony's creatures, some as high as sixteen feet, spilled into the streets, and the crowds cheered wildly.

Part puppet, part balloon, the air-filled rubber bags wobbled down the avenues, propped up by wooden sticks.

But now the sidewalks were so packed with people that only those in the first few rows could really see the parade. Tony realized his puppets would have to be even bigger and higher off the ground. And though the sticks helped to steer the puppets, they were stiff and heavy. Tony wanted his balloons to *articulate*—to move and gesture—more like puppets. But how?

With a marionette, the controls are above and the puppet hangs down...

BUT what if
the controls were
Below
and the
puppet
COULD
RiSE
UP?

During the next year, Tony set his new idea into motion.

This time, he asked the company in Ohio to make balloons out of rubberized silk—as strong as rubber but lighter than rubber alone.

Most important, Tony ordered the balloons to be filled not just with air but with helium too. Since helium is lighter than air, it would make the balloons rise.

Once the puppets were completed, they were deflated and shipped back to Tony in New York.

Tony did not know if everything would go as planned . . .

It was still dark on Thanksgiving morning when Tony filled the balloons with helium, tethering them down with sandbags.

By one p.m. the sidewalks were packed with people ready for the parade. Then, one by one, Tony cut the lines to the sandbags . . .

. . . and the magnificent upside-down marionettes
rose up to the skies!

Nodding and waving to the crowds below, they sailed past Central Park.
They sallied down Broadway.

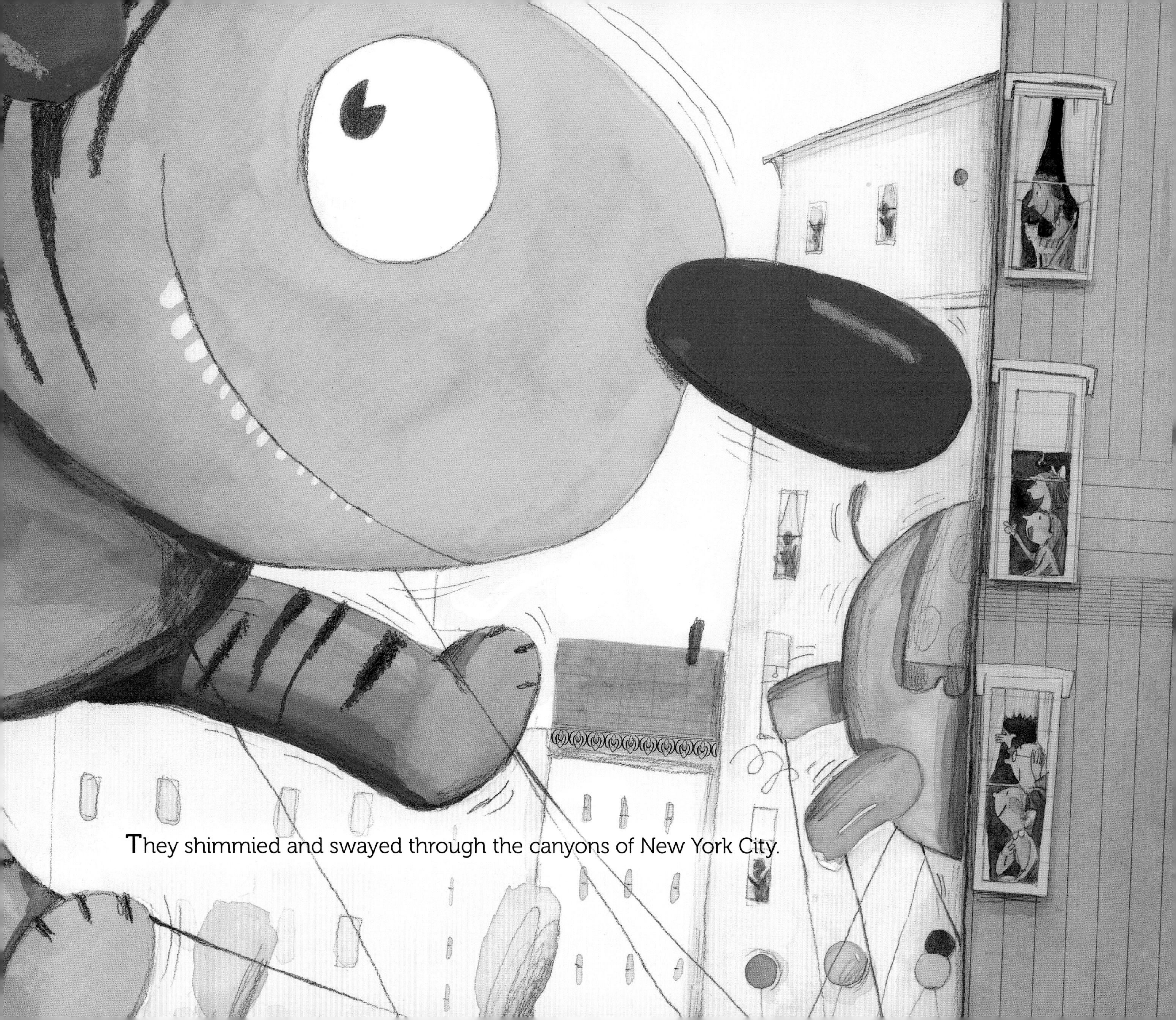

They shimmied and swayed through the canyons of New York City.

High above the crowds, they flounced in the afternoon wind, pulling the rope handlers this way and that. Yet with every heave-ho, the balloons gestured and articulated like wild puppets and the crowd screamed for more.

After the balloons were eased under the El, they ended in front of Macy's, at Tony's Wondertown windows.

It Was a PARADE NEW YORKers WOULD never forget!

And from that day on, every Thanksgiving morning, crowds have lined the sidewalks of New York City to see what new balloons would rise to the skies for Macy's famous parade.

Tony Sarg—the puppeteer who loved to figure out how to make things move—had set the stage, with a little rigging, for a puppet to be anything anyone could imagine it to be.

Author's Note

I have never done a stroke of work in my life. —TONY SARG

Tony Sarg clowning around in the Goodyear hangar.

Dear Tony Sarg,
Please send me one King, two Princesses, three Fairies and a Devil. I am sure Father will pay for them. Also a Dragon.

Tony Sarg's helium-filled balloons debuted in Macy's 1928 Thanksgiving Day Parade. Balloons have risen every year since, with the exception of two years during World War II when rubber and helium were needed in the war effort. Tony continued to work on the parade for many years, later collaborating with Walt Disney on the character balloons. Today, more than forty million people worldwide watch the parade, which is still imbued with the wit and humor of Tony Sarg.

Tony's daughter Mary once remarked, "Quite simply, Tony Sarg just never grew up." When he began making puppets, he relied on his childhood love of tinkering and figuring out how things worked. He taught himself how to carve wood, build sets, sew costumes, engineer electronics, and write plays. He had a keen attention to detail and made innovations to performing puppetry, elevating it to an art form that had not been seen before. Many consider Tony Sarg to be the father of American puppetry.

But Tony could not have accomplished all he did without his talented apprentices, some of whom went on to their own fame. One of his apprentices, Bil Baird, later created the puppets for the "Lonely Goatherd" marionette show featured in the movie *The Sound of Music.* (And one of Baird's apprentices was Jim Henson, who invented the Muppets.)

Even with no formal art lessons, Tony became one of the busiest artists of his day. But whether he was illustrating his children's books, designing toys, creating animations, or managing his marionette troupe as it crisscrossed the country, Tony still made time for children. They were his favorite audience. He responded to every letter he received, one of which was simply addressed "Tony Sarg, N.Y."

A FEW WORDS ABOUT THE ART

To create the art for this book, I began by making toys and puppets. I played with all sorts of materials, not knowing exactly what the outcome would be. In addition to the watercolor illustrations, my collages are, in part, a mix of paper from old books to make papier-mâché puppets, found objects, and fabrics, all painted or altered to illustrate what it may have felt like to be in Sarg's world. Some of the toys in my illustrations are based on ones from Tony's vast collection, but the actual toys in this book are ones I made. On a few of the pages I even used Tony's illustrations from *The Tony Sarg Marionette Book.* I tried to keep in mind that in everything Sarg did, he conveyed the sense that he was having fun. His legacy reminds me that "play" may be the most important element in making art!

To Tony Sarg and his cast of Characters

Thank you to everyone who spoke to me about Tony Sarg. For your kindness and generosity, I tip my hat to John Bell and Bart Roccoberton of the Ballard Institute and Museum of Puppetry; the Nantucket Historical Association; Rachelle Stern, Macy's senior counsel; Bill Smith, balloon designer at Balloonworks; Robert Grippo, Rod Hook, George Korn, Andrew Pfeiffer, Bob Rutan, Mia Galison, and Sax Freymann of eeBoo Toys; Rachel Newborn, art director, and my editor, Ann Rider. And a big applause to my family, who listened as I regaled them with stories of Tony Sarg through countless suppertimes.

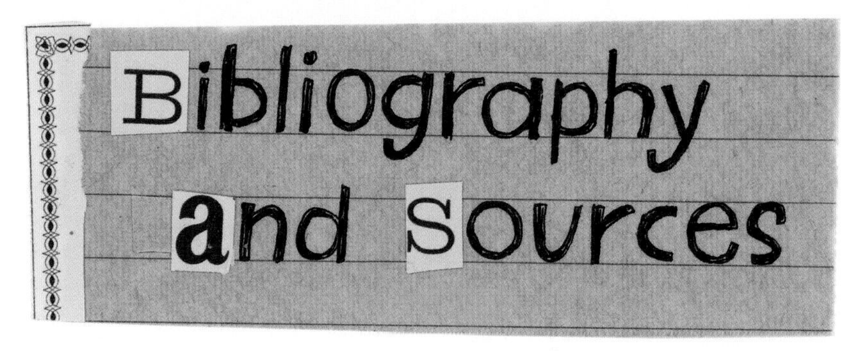

Allen, Hugh. *The House of Goodyear: Fifty Years of Men and Industry.* Cleveland, Ohio: Corday & Gross, 1949.

Baird, Bil. *The Art of the Puppet.* New York: Bonanza Books, 1973.

The Ballard Institute and Museum of Puppetry, www.bimp.uconn.edu

Bird, William L., Jr. *Holidays on Display.* New York: Princeton Architectural Press, 2007.

Blumenthal, Eileen. *Puppetry: A World History.* New York: Abrams, 2005.

Corey, Shana. *Milly and the Macy's Day Parade.* New York: Scholastic, 2002.

Grippo, Robert. *Macy's Thanksgiving Day Parade.* Charleston, S.C.: Arcadia Publishing, 2004.

Hunt, Tamara Robin. *Tony Sarg: Puppeteer in America, 1915–1942.* North Vancouver, B.C.: Charlemagne Press, 1988.

Inside Macy's Thanksgiving Day Parade. DVD. History Channel, 2009.

Macy's Inc., www.macys.com/campaign/parade/history.jsp

Madden, Stephen. *America's Parade: A Celebration of Macy's Thanksgiving Day Parade.* New York: Time, 2001.

Mazzarella, Mark, director. *Stories of the American Puppet.* DVD. Mazzarella Media, 2007.

McIsaac, F. J. *The Tony Sarg Marionette Book.* New York: B. W. Huebsch, 1921.

The Nantucket Historical Association, www.nha.org

Sarg, Tony. Papers, 1904–1963. Smithsonian Archives for American Art, Washington, D.C.

———. *Tony Sarg's New York.* New York: Greenberg Publisher, 1926.

———. "Tony Sarg Takes a Look at New York Life." *New York Times Magazine,* September 27, 1945.

Saunders, John Monk. "Tony Sarg Has Never Done a Stroke of Work in His Life!" *American Magazine,* May 1926, 107.

QUOTE SOURCES

"Every little movement has a meaning of its own." Sarg, "Takes a Look."

"I have never done a stroke of work in my life." Hunt, *Puppeteer in America.* (Hunt's source is Saunders, "Tony Sarg Has Never.")

"Quite frankly, Tony Sarg just never grew up." Robert Benchley, "Tony Sarg's Colorful Career Recalled by His Daughter," *Nantucket Inquirer and Mirror,* August 18, 1983.

"Dear Tony Sarg . . ." Hunt, *Puppeteer in America.*

Photos courtesy of the Nantucket Historical Association, PH8274 and PH8941.

Original advertisement from the New York Times, 1933, courtesy of Macy's Inc.

cated
Roosev

E MONEY TO BE ASKED

s Ordered to Survey Needs r Congress, With Continu- ing Projects in Mind.

Special to THE NEW YORK TIMES.
WARM SPRINGS, Ga., Nov. 29. The $3,300,000,000 public works nd, of which only about $150,000,- 0 remains unallocated or not ear- marked, will be completely disposed f within three weeks, it was an- nounced at the "Winter White House" today.

The available funds in that relief reservoir appropriated by the last session of Congress shrank by $250,- 000,000 during the four-day visit

e of Secretary Ickes, but details projects approved were not made lic here.

While in conference with the Pub- Works Administrator President oosevelt carefully checked over

to July penditures betw July 1, 1935, and t nce which will remai thereafter.

Further studies have been or- dered by the President to determine how much money Congress will be asked for to further authorized works for which only enough money was allocated to carry them up to the end of this fiscal year.

The public works for which funds have been supplied or obligated are of all varieties, ranging from Fed- eral construction to projects as not yet defined in detail, such as the Triborough Bridge in New York.

In the case of actual Federal con- struction, public works funds have been allocated only for the current fiscal year and further appropria- tions will be required in succeeding years to carry on. Such a project is the channel work authorized on the upper Mississippi River.

The Triborough Bridge, on the other hand, is a self-liquidating work projected by a public corpora- tion, the Port of New York ity, for which it is esti 000,000 to $36,000,000 quired, and all of w earmarked in the fund now, although be expended over pr year period.

tributes Q of League Comm

Wireless to THE NEW Y
LA PAZ, Bolivia, N visit of the League of mission to the Chaco to have brought an to the Bolivian an armies for bulletins livian command have "unimportant events than a week.

This is taken here that a survey by the m bers of the commission General Robertson and General Freydenberg, n Casado on the Paragu keeping the Paraguaya busy.

However, official Bolivi assert the lull is due also to of the last Paraguayan offensive.

E SILK STRIKE PATERSON

Return to y After eeks.

AY RISE

t Wages After stry.

TIMES. . 29.—The for four- e industry when or- mally ap- The agree- ay and the the mills settlement workers in

ent that the vas made this Greene, impar- he joint confer- which earlier in the terms on which the settlement was based. Mr. Greene's announcement was made to 4,000 workers who had gathered in front of the City Hall Annex, where the workers' ballots were counted today.

The peace terms provide for union recognition, a forty-hour week and $2 per 100,000 picks for weavers; pickers, $14 a week; loom fixers, $15; quillers, $14.40; warpers, 13 to 14½ cents per 1,000 ends, 100 yards; twisters, 52 to 85 cents per 1,000 ends; machine twisting, 25 cents per 1,000 ends, and entering, 90 cents to $1.10 per 1,000 ends. This approximates a 15 per cent increase over the old scale.

The agreement provides for the appointment of an industrial relations board, composed of three unionists, three manufacturers and an impartial chairman. The board will be charged with preventing future strikes and every sixty days will make a survey of the entire silk industry to determine the average wage in the two highest paying silk districts outside of Paterson. Manufacturers here have agreed to pay 5 per cent higher than this average and the industrial relations board will have the power to revise wage schedules every sixty days accordingly.

The pact, which is for a year, will be signed for the workers by the Associated Silk Workers, unit of the American Federation of Silk Workers; the Horizontal Workers Protective Association, the Loom Fixers and Twisters Protective and Benevolent and the United Wa

The bros arted in Paterson a eks had become na bringing out at its stimated to number in New Jersey, N England and Penn of the sections c already have retur hose still out are e ge peace terms on those ap- proved he

The bro nt is the second of ce in the general s silk dyers having se ences four weeks ag remain on strike a bout 2,500 silk thro expected to negoti soon.

Woma ntempt.

Mrs. C rtlett, first wife of lo-Bartlett, said to police in Cuba, w ontempt of court y homas W. Churchi rt referee, because nswer ques- tions in Doris Abelo- Bartlett e, to annul her ma round that the de legal wife when h ast Septem- ber. The sed to testify as to her alleged marriage and of the possibilit she had been divorced.

!! HERE COMES THE PARADE!!

IT'S IMMENSE! IT'S COLOSSAL! *COME A-RUNNIN !*

THE TIME? Today. Thanksgiving Day. 2:00 o'clock sharp it starts. Rain or shine. Don't be late! At approximately 4:30 Santa Claus will unveil Macy's Christmas Toy windows.

THE PLACE? Straight down Broadway from 110th Street to 34th. Miles of fun and frolic. Fabulous floats ... booming bands ... capering clowns ... it's a riot ... bring the kids!

SEE THEM! HEAR THEM! TONY SARG'S

Helium Filled Monsters

!!!!!!!!

He laughs like a thousand men!

GULLIVER THE GULLIBLE

He peeps in eighth story windows ... believes what he sees ... and laughs while he looks. Takes 40 men to hold him. The Greatest Gas Bag in History!

Oink! Oink! Here Comes